managing
pressure
in your marriage

homebuilders
COUPLES SERIES®

managing
pressure
in your marriage

by
dennis rainey
&
robert lewis

Little Rock, Arkansas

MANAGING PRESSURE IN YOUR MARRIAGE
FamilyLife Publishing®
5800 Ranch Drive
Little Rock, Arkansas 72223
1-800-FL-TODAY • FamilyLife.com

FLTI, d/b/a FamilyLife®, is a ministry of Campus Crusade for Christ International®

ISBN: 978-1-60200-334-7

Design: Brand Navigation, LLC

Cover image: © Getty Images/MIXA

Printed in the United States of America

14 13 12 11 10   2 3 4 5

Unless the LORD builds the house,
those who build it labor in vain.

PSALM 127:1

The HomeBuilders Couples Series®

Building Your Marriage to Last
Improving Communication in Your Marriage
Resolving Conflict in Your Marriage
Mastering Money in Your Marriage
Building Teamwork in Your Marriage
Growing Together in Christ
Building Up Your Spouse
Managing Pressure in Your Marriage

The HomeBuilders Parenting Series®

Improving Your Parenting
Establishing Effective Discipline for Your Children
Guiding Your Teenagers
Raising Children of Faith

Marriage should be enjoyed, not endured. It is meant to be a vibrant relationship between two people who love each other with passion, commitment, understanding, and grace. So secure is the bond God desires between a husband and a wife that he uses it to illustrate the magnitude of Christ's love for the church (Ephesians 5:25–33).

Do you have that kind of love in your marriage?

Relationships often fade over time as people drift apart—but only if the relationship is left unattended. We have a choice in the matter; our marriages don't have to grow dull. Perhaps we just need to give them some attention.

That's the purpose behind the HomeBuilders Couples Series—to provide you a way to give your marriage the attention it needs and deserves. This is a biblically based small-group study because, in the Bible, God has given the blueprint for building a loving and secure marriage. His plan is designed to enable a man and a woman to grow together in a mutually satisfying relationship and then to reach out to others with the love of Christ. Ignoring God's plan may lead to isolation and, in far too many cases, the breakup of the home.

Whether your marriage needs a complete makeover or just a few small adjustments, we encourage you to consult God's design. Although written nearly two thousand years ago, Scripture still speaks clearly and powerfully about the conflicts and challenges men and women face.

Do we really need to be part of a group? Couldn't we just go through this study as a couple?

While you could work through the study as a couple, you would miss the opportunity to connect with friends and to learn from one another's experiences. You will find that the questions in each session not only help you grow closer to your spouse, but they also create an environment of warmth and fellowship with other couples as you study together.

What does it take to lead a HomeBuilders group?

Leading a group is much easier than you may think, because the leader is simply a facilitator who guides the participants through the discussion questions. You are not teaching the material but are helping the couples discover and apply biblical truths. The special dynamic of a HomeBuilders group is that couples teach themselves.

The study guide you're holding has all the information and guidance you need to participate in or lead a HomeBuilders group. You'll find leader's notes in the back of the guide, and additional helps are posted online at FamilyLife.com/HomeBuilders.

What is the typical schedule?

Most studies in the HomeBuilders Couples Series are six to eight weeks long, indicated by the number of sessions in the guide. The sessions are designed to take sixty minutes in the group with a project for the couples to complete between sessions.

Isn't it risky to talk about your marriage in a group?

The group setting should be enjoyable and informative—and non-threatening. THREE SIMPLE GROUND RULES will help ensure that everyone feels comfortable and gets the most out of the experience:

1. Share nothing that will embarrass your spouse.
2. You may pass on any question you do not want to answer.
3. If possible, as a couple complete the HomeBuilders project between group sessions.

What other help does FamilyLife offer?

Our list of marriage and family resources continues to grow. Visit FamilyLife.com to learn more about our:

- Weekend to Remember® getaway and other events;
- slate of radio broadcasts, including the nationally syndicated *FamilyLife Today*®, *Real FamilyLife with Dennis Rainey*®, and *FamilyLife This Week*®;
- multimedia resources for small groups, churches, and community networking;
- interactive products for parents, couples, small-group leaders, and one-to-one mentors; and
- assortment of blogs, forums, and other online connections.

Dennis Rainey is the president and a cofounder of FamilyLife (a ministry of Campus Crusade for Christ) and a graduate of Dallas Theological Seminary. For more than thirty-five years, he has been speaking and writing on marriage and family issues. Since 1976, he has overseen the development of FamilyLife's numerous outreaches, including the popular Weekend to Remember marriage getaway. He is also the daily host of the nationally syndicated radio program *FamilyLife Today*. He and his wife, Barbara, have six children and sixteen grandchildren.

Robert Lewis is president and executive producer of LifeReady, an organization that provides high-impact video resources to prepare couples, parents, men, and women to embrace God's best for their marriages, families, and lives. He has authored numerous books and films, including the nationally recognized Men's Fraternity series: *Quest for Authentic Manhood, Winning at Work and Home,* and *The Great Adventure.* Robert serves on the board of trustees for Leadership Network. Married since 1971, Robert and his wife, Sherard, reside in Little Rock, Arkansas, and have four children and two grandchildren.

contents

All of us face pressure. Some of it is just the natural stuff of everyday life. But some of it is brought upon us by our lack of planning, poor choices, wrong values, unresolved conflicts, and leaving God out of our lives.

We want to help you reduce pressure by addressing common problems in some fresh new ways, using the timeless truths of Scripture. *Managing Pressure in Your Marriage* will help you as a couple come to grips with how you make decisions, how you agree on moral boundaries, and how you face new seasons in your life and thus new issues and problems in your marriage. This study won't provide you with all the answers, but it will aid you in hammering out your own convictions and solutions as you navigate life's circumstances.

Enjoy these sessions. Do the projects. Talk. Interact. Hammer out what you believe, based on God's Word. But, regardless, get involved with your spouse in addressing six of life's most pressing issues. We know the end result will be worth it!

—Dennis & Barbara Rainey

1

Decision Making and Pressure

Making wise decisions is essential in resolving the pressures that life brings.

warm-up

1. Choose one of the following questions to answer:

- What is something funny or unique that happened at your wedding or on your honeymoon?

- Think back over the past twelve months. What have been some highlights of your year, and why?

2. What do you hope to get out of this study?

Living in a Pressure-Cooker World

1. What are some circumstances or expectations that cause you to feel pressure and stress during a typical week—at work or at home?

2. How do you typically react to pressure? How does it affect you physically and emotionally?

Case Study: How Decisions Affect the Pressure We Experience

Ryan and Melissa enjoyed their life in the midwestern town where they had both grown up. Ryan managed the local office of a national insurance firm and did it well. He didn't earn a large salary, but housing in their town was pretty inexpensive, so his income was enough to allow Melissa to stay home with their two young children. They belonged to a church they both enjoyed, and their parents lived within ten minutes of them.

Then Ryan received a visit from his district manager. "I'm moving to the corporate office in New York," the manager said. "I need to find a replacement, and you're my first choice."

For Ryan, this seemed like the opportunity of a lifetime. The new position would mean a substantial increase in salary and would even give him the opportunity to do some traveling. The only drawback was that the family would have to move to Houston, several hundred miles away. Ryan knew he would miss his family and friends, but he was excited about the prospect of advancing his career.

Melissa protested that she didn't want to leave. "I'm happy here. I don't want to leave my family and friends."

"But we'll never have the chance to get ahead if we stay here," Ryan argued. "This way we can afford to get a larger house. We'll be able to sell our old car and get an SUV. And with the kids getting bigger, you know we need one."

Eventually Ryan won her over. Three months later they found themselves in a new home, a new city, and a new SUV. But now they were facing a new set of problems they hadn't anticipated.

First, there was the job, which turned out to require more than a little traveling. Ryan was often out of town three or four days each week, and he needed to work many Saturdays. Melissa sometimes felt like a single mother, and it seemed worse because she was unable to lean on her family to help with the kids as she had before. On top of that, she became pregnant again.

They missed their families and their friends terribly. They joined a good church, but Ryan was often so tired on Sunday that he just wanted to sleep in. And he was out of town so often on weekday nights that they decided they couldn't commit to joining a couples' Bible study.

Their new life went on like this for a year, and then came the big bombshell: Ryan's company was sold to a larger conglomerate that already had a district manager in that area. Ryan's work was highly regarded by his new employers, however, and once again he was offered a new position—as a regional manager working out of Atlanta. "We need people like you, Ryan," he was told. "In a few years you'll probably be moving up to the New York office."

3. What pressures were Ryan and Melissa feeling as they made their first decision about moving?

4. In what ways did Ryan and Melissa's decision increase the pressures they felt?

5. What factors should Ryan and Melissa consider as they decide whether to move to Atlanta?

Much of the pressure we feel each day is unavoidable—it's part of life. But the decisions we make in response to the situations that cause pressure are critical. We can make decisions that reduce pressure and help us cope with it, or we can make decisions that increase the pressure beyond what we're presently feeling.

 homebuilders principle: Good decisions can make pressure reasonable and bearable.

Principles of Good Decision Making

In our lives all of us will make countless decisions that set our direction, reveal our values, and determine our course. Decisions determine our destiny and play a key role in how we handle the pressures we face each day. Yet few people ever receive formal training in how to make good decisions. Even fewer take the time to hammer out a biblically based strategy for decision making—one that is based on how God wants us to make our choices.

Principle 1: Put God first.

6. Read Matthew 6:33–34. How would you apply this truth to decision making?

homebuilders principle: Our decisions mirror our values; they should reflect our desire to put God first in our lives.

Principle 2: Obey the Scriptures.

7. What does Matthew 7:24–27 say about the foundation for our decisions? How can this affect the pressures you face in your marriage and family life?

Principle 3: Seek God's wisdom—together.

For some decisions you may not be able to find a verse or passage from Scripture that provides clear guidance. When this happens, you will need to seek the Lord together as a couple and ask for wisdom. This involves four steps:

- Praying for guidance (Proverbs 3:5–7)
- Honestly evaluating your options (Luke 14:28–32)
- Seeking wise counsel (Proverbs 12:15; 13:20; 15:22)
- Deciding which of your choices is the wisest, and committing your decision together to God

8. Read Ecclesiastes 4:9–12. Why are you better off making your decisions together as a couple?

9. What is an example of a good decision you have made together as a couple?

homebuilders principle: Wise decisions are born from wise counsel—from God and the Scriptures and from godly advisers—and from prayer together as a couple.

To manage pressure in marriage, it's essential that a couple understands and practices good decision making. You can use the principles learned in this session for a multitude of decisions in your life.

In the remaining sessions you will study five crucial areas that place enormous pressure on families today. If they are not handled properly, they can crush a marriage relationship.

make a date

Set a time for you and your spouse to complete the HomeBuilders project together before the next group meeting. You will be asked at the next session to share an insight or experience from the project.

date _____ time _____

location _____

homebuilders project

On Your Own

Answer the following questions:

1. Review session 1, and write down the most important concept or truth you learned.

2. As you grew up, what did you observe about the way your parents made decisions?

3. How do you and your spouse differ in the way you make decisions?

4. Take a look at the principles for decision making outlined in the Blueprints section. What do you think are your greatest strengths and weaknesses in this area?

5. What action do you need to take to improve your decision-making ability? (For example, have a daily prayer time, involve your spouse more in decisions, etc.)

6. In your opinion, what are your spouse's greatest strengths and weaknesses in decision making?

7. What two or three pressures are you currently facing that a wise decision might take away?

8. Have you made any decisions lately that you need to reevaluate—choices that have placed additional pressure on you, your spouse, or your family? If so, list them.

9. What is one thing you'd like to implement in your marriage as a result of this study?

With Your Spouse

1. Share your responses to the questions you answered on your own.

2. As you look at the subject of decision making, discuss the following:

   - What is one thing we're doing *right* as a couple?

   - What is one thing we need to *stop* doing?

   - What is one thing we need to *start* doing?

3. Consider your typical weekly schedule. What decisions could you make to alleviate some of the time pressure you may feel?

4. Close in prayer together. Pray for each other, for wisdom, and for any decisions you need to make.

Remember to take your calendar to the next session for Make a Date.

2

The Pressure of
Materialism

Couples can reduce pressure in their marriages by taking a hard look at how they make financial decisions.

warm-up

1. Choose one of the following:

   - Tell about something foolish you've seen or heard that other people do with money.
   - Share something foolish you've done with your money.
   - Share a childhood scheme that you had for making money. What was the result?

2. Why do you think so many couples say that finances are a major source of pressure in their marriages?

3. How have you experienced pressure as a couple as you have managed your financial resources? If you are willing, tell about your first conflict over money or a recent difficult discussion you had regarding money.

Project Report

If you completed the HomeBuilders project from the first session, share one thing you learned.

The Causes and Results of Materialism

Couples can do many things to improve their money-management skills. They would be wise to begin by taking a hard look at the materialistic attitudes that often lead to poor financial decisions.

The second college edition of *Webster's New World Dictionary* provides some interesting definitions of the word *materialism*: "the doctrine that comfort, pleasure, and wealth are the only or highest goals or values . . . the tendency to be more concerned with material than with spiritual or intellectual goals or values."

1. What are some indications of a materialistic attitude?

2. Why is it so easy to be materialistic in our culture?

3. Read the following case study.

Case Study

Like many young couples, Robert and Maria began their married life in an apartment. During their first four years of marriage, they both worked, and eventually they managed to save enough money for a small down payment on their own home. Soon after Maria gave birth to their first child, they purchased a three-bedroom home in a neighborhood where quite a few other young couples lived. The house was not especially large, but it was adequate for their needs. They wanted to live on one income, and they were able to do that with this house.

During the next several years, Robert and Maria had two more children, and they enjoyed refurbishing the home. Robert continued to take on more responsibility at work, and his income increased accordingly. When their youngest child entered kindergarten, Maria decided to take a part-time job as a preschool teacher.

After they had been in the home for nine years, Robert and Maria became a bit restless. "This house is starting to feel small," Maria said. "The kids could use more room to play and entertain their friends."

It seemed as if all the couples they knew were moving into bigger homes. "You should see the house that the Spragues moved into," Robert said. "Just walking through it made me jealous!"

Robert and Maria spent a few weekends with a Realtor and came upon the house of their dreams. It had just been built, and it offered four bedrooms, thirty-five hundred square feet, a sunroom, a huge backyard, crown molding throughout the house, and brand-new appliances in the kitchen.

The first problem was the price. Their house payment would more than double, and the only way they could afford that would be for Maria to find a new job with more hours. Their budget would be pretty tight, but they were convinced that the house would be worth any sacrifice. "This is the home I've always wanted," Maria said. "I just know we'll be happy here."

The second problem was their furniture. "We can't move into a nice home like this and keep our old stuff," Robert said. "It's embarrassing." With their tight budget, they didn't have cash to buy new furniture for the living room, dining room, and kids' bedrooms. They didn't have enough cash to purchase the large-screen television Robert wanted for the family room. So they decided to buy it on credit. They vowed they would pay it all off within the next eighteen months.

- What were some of the attitudes and pressures that led Robert and Maria to purchase the larger home?

- What kinds of pressures are they likely to experience as a result of this decision?

• How did Robert and Maria's decision reflect their values?

4. In what ways has the tendency to compare yourself with others affected you and your financial decisions?

5. What do the following scriptures say about materialism and handling money?

• Matthew 13:18–23 (especially verse 22)

• Luke 12:15–21

• 1 Timothy 6:6–10

6. What are common ways that we rationalize materialistic attitudes?

homebuilders principle: Couples need to seek contentment within the means that God has provided.

Looking at Your Values

7. Read Matthew 6:33. How can you practically apply this principle when making financial decisions?

8. Look again at 1 Timothy 6:6–10, and this time add verses 11 and 12. What advice do you find, especially in these last two verses, that would help you avoid materialism's grip?

9. How can determining what true success means help in conquering materialism?

A key to making good decisions that will reduce the pressures on your financial situation is simply to be honest with yourself. Here are a few questions you can use when making financial decisions:

- Am I seeking contentment in this purchase?
- Is this a need or a want?
- Have we prayed about this purchase and discussed it as a couple?
- Will the purchase please God?
- Will it create additional pressure over the next one to five years?
- Will it cause us to go into debt?
- Will our family relationships suffer because of this decision?

make a date

Set a time for you and your spouse to complete the HomeBuilders project together before the next group meeting. You will be asked at the next session to share an insight or experience from the project.

date _____ time _____

location _____

homebuilders project

On Your Own

Answer the following questions:

1. Complete the following exercise:

MATERIALISM: A SELF-APPRAISAL

	Strongly Disagree		Undecided		Strongly Agree
a. I would be happier if I could double my income.	1	2	3	4	5
b. I really love buying things.	1	2	3	4	5
c. I find myself often thinking about things I'd like to buy.	1	2	3	4	5
d. My car makes me feel good about myself.	1	2	3	4	5
e. My self-worth is tied to how my home looks.	1	2	3	4	5
f. I have a long list of things I wish I could buy.	1	2	3	4	5
g. I spend a great deal of emotional and mental energy thinking of or finding things I'd like to buy.	1	2	3	4	5

	Strongly Disagree		Undecided		Strongly Agree
h. My kids are preoccupied with things they want.	1	2	3	4	5
i. My closet is full of nice clothes that I don't wear because they're out of style.	1	2	3	4	5
j. We would give more to church or charities if we could better control our spending.	1	2	3	4	5
k. **Husbands:** I would be willing for my wife to stay at home with our children if it didn't mean a significant drop in our income.	1	2	3	4	5
Wives: I would be willing to stay at home with our children if it didn't mean a significant drop in our income.	1	2	3	4	5
l. We would be in full-time ministry if it didn't involve a sacrificial lifestyle.	1	2	3	4	5
m. Other people's opinions of my lifestyle matter a lot to me.	1	2	3	4	5

2. From this appraisal, what conclusions do you draw about your success as a couple in resisting materialism and its pressures?

3. Answer if applicable: How would you evaluate your success in raising children who resist materialism and its pressures? Why?

4. What decisions from the past are putting pressure on you and your spouse today? Are there any decisions you can make today that would reduce the pressure?

5. Reread Matthew 6:33 and 1 Timothy 6:6–12. What might God be saying to you or your family through these passages?

With Your Spouse

1. Share your responses to the questions you answered on your own.

2. As a couple how can you work together to reduce or avoid future pressure from materialism?

3. If you can, write down one or two action points that could reduce pressure in your marriage and family.

4. Close your time together with prayer, asking God for the wisdom and strength to make sound decisions about your finances.

Remember to take your calendar to the next session for Make a Date.

3

The Pressure of
Weariness

Weariness may have less to do with the amount of work and number of activities a couple is involved with and more to do with a lack of the right kind of rest.

How would you assess your feelings about the pace of your lifestyle? In the list of words below, circle two that most accurately describe you right now.

Discouraged
Relaxed
Exhausted
Organized
Hopeful
Energetic

Out of control

Peaceful

Panicky

Cruising

Ragged

Disorganized

Adjusting

Encouraged

Worthless

Tired

Pressured

Strung out

Share your two choices with the group. Tell why you picked them.

Project Report

Share one thing you learned from the HomeBuilders project from last session.

The Problem of Weariness in Your Marriage

Weariness is a pressure that afflicts many marriages in our highly mobile, fast-paced society. Of course, some of our fatigue is understandable and unavoidable. But other weariness results from our choices.

1. How can you tell when your spouse is weary? What are the warning signs?

2. In what ways do you think weariness has affected the quality of your marriage?

3. What habits or routines have you established as a couple to protect your marriage from burnout?

Rest Stop 1: Refocusing

Few things are as exhausting as racing through life without a clear sense of purpose and direction. To feel pulled by a packed schedule can be tiring, but to see no real purpose in all that activity can expand a natural sense of weariness into an unnatural, soul-numbing exhaustion.

We need to take time to make sense out of all that is happening to us. This is what *refocusing* means. Refocusing pumps meaning and direction back into a person's and a couple's activities by asking basic questions like these:

- Why are we driving ourselves like this?
- Where is all this taking us?
- What impact does all this activity have on our marriage?
- Is God pleased with the things we are involved in?
- What are our most important priorities?
- Can we let anything go?

4. When was the last time, in an unhurried atmosphere, that you and your spouse challenged each other's schedules with questions like those listed above?

 homebuilders principle: Nothing is as wearisome as wandering through life.

Rest Stop 2: Releasing

When you release things that seem important and feel important but really are not, you can experience almost instant refreshment.

5. Read Luke 10:38–42. What kinds of avoidable pressures was Jesus trying to get Martha to release? How did he help her get a more accurate perspective?

6. What are some past activities and concerns that exhausted both your life and marriage and that you now know were actually unnecessary?

7. What decisions could you make to decrease current responsibilities, expectations, or commitments that weigh you down?

homebuilders principle: In some areas of life, letting go may be the best strategy. Couples can decrease pressure in their lives by deciding to cut down on their responsibilities, expectations, and commitments.

Rest Stop 3: Repentance

8. At first it may seem odd that repentance can be coupled with rest. And yet, what does Psalm 32:3–5 tell us about the effect of unconfessed sin?

9. What are some ways people expend great amounts of time and energy seeking to conceal or make excuses for sinful behaviors?

10. In what ways has humble confession saved you and your spouse from pain and conserved your energy for your marriage?

homebuilders principle: Unacknowledged sin has a price—exhaustion! Real rest is found in having a clear conscience.

make a date

Set a time for you and your spouse to complete the HomeBuilders project together before the next group meeting. You will be asked at the next session to share an insight or experience from the project.

date _____ time _____

location _____

homebuilders project

On Your Own

Answer the following questions:

1. Review Rest Stop 2 from the Blueprints section. Reread the scripture recommended there. What things could you release as a couple in order to ease pressure in your family?

2. Read Psalm 139:23–24. Does this statement by David express the desire of your own heart? If so, ask God honestly, "What sin am I not facing up to that is wearing me out?" Sit in silence before him, and list below those answers that surface in your conscience.

3. Now read 1 John 1:9. Do you believe this statement? If so . . .

   • Confess to God right now what you have recorded in the space above. Tell him each item specifically. Admit that

these things are wrong and that you want to change.
Now thank God that he has forgiven you for these
wrongdoings. Before God, you are now forgiven. Clean!

- As a gesture of your faith, draw an X across the sins you
listed, then write the word *Forgiven.* Because of your
confession, God no longer holds these sins against you.
Rejoice and be thankful!

Close this time in prayer, asking God's help in those areas where you
have previously failed. You might also determine now to seek the
counsel and help of others to address the weaknesses of your life.

With Your Spouse

1. What did Jesus mean when he said, "The Sabbath was made
for man" (Mark 2:27)? "Made for man" to do what?

2. What role does Sunday play in your weekly schedule? Check
one:

- It's a day like any other day.
- It's a day to catch up.
- It's a day to relax.
- It's a day for recreation.
- It's a day to worship and evaluate.
- Other:

3. What steps could you take to make Sunday a more meaning-ful rest day and a cure for the exhaustion of unclear living and purposeless activity?

4. Using a pencil (so you can erase), write down all the major events and activities that will consume your time over the next two months. Also list recurring items and regular meet-ings that you may not think of as events (choir practice, daily run, etc.).

5. Fill out the following chart together. Be sure to listen to each other; often your spouse can see what is unnecessary in your life better than you can.

   Unnecessary things we can let go of:

Unnecessary things in my life:

Unnecessary things in my spouse's life:

Unnecessary things we do together:

6. What action steps must you take to let go of unnecessary activities and commitments in your life together?

7. What conflicts surface between you as you ask these questions? Seek to resolve these differences with mutual understanding and love.

8. Commit to refocus again in six weeks. Remember: nothing is as wearisome as wandering through life.

9. Close in prayer.

Remember to take your calendar to the next session for Make a Date.

4

Seasonal Pressures

A wise couple will prepare for the special seasons of marriage and their unique challenges.

warm-up

Case Study

Jason and Amy would say that the first five years of their marriage were excellent. During that time Jason settled into a well-paying job while Amy taught elementary school. They were able to purchase a comfortable three-bedroom home that, even now, meets their needs.

Recently they celebrated their ninth anniversary but with little joy. Their marriage feels different now. Last year Amy left teaching after having her second child. She enjoys being at home with her children, but often she feels exhausted from continual, relentless responsibility. She is starved for adult conversation. And she doesn't feel she is accomplishing as much with her life as she once did.

Jason has experienced a major change too. Since his promotion to regional manager, he is traveling much more, and he often works longer hours. Jason also continues to play basketball every weekend, and although Amy complains, he feels he deserves some time off.

Amy feels Jason is not involved enough with her and the children. Jason, on the other hand, believes he does all he can. He sometimes resents feeling that he is competing with the kids for Amy's affection.

Both Jason and Amy sense a growing isolation from each other. They're surprised at the sudden flashes of anger they have felt. Their excellent marriage has turned sour. As their resentment builds, they are frightened to think they may be falling out of love.

1. How would you summarize this couple's problem?

2. How would you advise Jason and Amy? What adjustments do they need to make in this new season of their life together? What new commitments would you say they need to make to each other to recapture the success they enjoyed in the first five years of their marriage?

An Overall Perspective

Every marriage goes through a series of distinct phases or seasons. By *season,* we mean a specific time period in which certain events, issues, adjustments, and needs are typical and clearly different from those in other periods of the marriage.

Most people recognize that their lives proceed in distinct stages—for example, the teenage years, young adulthood, and middle age. Marriages, too, have distinct phases, and each one is like a marriage within a marriage. Every season requires fresh perspectives, new commitments, and a special kind of preparation from each spouse to successfully walk through it.

1. What season is your marriage in right now? What seasons has it already passed through?

Many couples are not prepared for the pressures they will face when they enter a new season in their marriages. In the same way that many couples begin marriage with little idea of what faces them, many begin each season of their married lives with little thought or understanding of what lies ahead. As a result, it's easy to be surprised and even overwhelmed by the unique pressures.

2. As you look back now, what kinds of issues do you wish you had been prepared for as you started your marriage?

3. How well prepared were you for dealing with your present season of life?

4. How can you apply the following verses to the principle of understanding different seasons of marriage and preparing for them in advance?

- Proverbs 24:3–4

- Luke 14:28–30

homebuilders principle: Advance preparation is the best pressure-release valve for a new marital season.

The Seasons of Marriage

In some ways marriage seasons are not difficult to determine. And yet it may not be easy to recognize the distinct pressures of each and what adjustments must be made to counter such pressures. The better a couple prepares for a marital season, the more advantages they will have as they try to manage the unique pressures that season brings.

The following chart shows the seasons that most marriages move through, along with typical pressing issues that couples face in each season. As you read through these and discuss them, feel free to add other issues you feel are relevant.

NEWLY MARRIED

- Defining and agreeing on your new roles as husband and wife—who does what
- Developing a relationship with in-laws
- Learning how to get along on a daily basis
- Learning how to communicate and resolve conflict
- Adjusting to differences: values, tastes, needs, etc.
- Other:

MARRIED WITH PRESCHOOLERS

- Making major decisions concerning careers and children
- Maintaining time for each other and not losing touch
- Developing new roles and accepting new responsibilities as you begin raising children
- Handling the money squeeze
- Keeping the relationship fresh
- Coping with growing responsibilities at work
- Other:

GROWING MARRIAGE; SCHOOL-AGE CHILDREN

- Juggling the pace of your expanding responsibilities
- Maintaining sanity in your schedule as your children begin school, add new friends, and begin activities of their own
- Handling the increasing money squeeze with savings, college, and retirement concerns
- Adjusting to teenagers
- Keeping romance alive after ten to twenty years of marriage
- Other:

MATURE MARRIED LIFE; LAUNCHING AND RELEASING CHILDREN

- Handling midlife crises
- Dealing with aging and ill parents
- Coping with increasing health concerns
- Managing money pressures with children in college
- Releasing children successfully into the adult world
- Other:

MARRIAGE IN TRANSITION; EMPTY NEST

- Adjusting to new roles for both husband and wife after children
- Refocusing on the marriage relationship
- Developing a new lifestyle
- Allocating resources for future needs
- Changing the relationship with children as they marry and begin families of their own
- Defining roles as in-laws and grandparents
- Other:

MARRIAGE IN RETIREMENT

- Dealing with health setbacks
- Finding a new purpose after retiring from work
- Adjusting to retirement income
- Other:

5. What seasons do the couples in your group fall into?

6. Share with the group what has helped you the most in handling the season of life you are now in (or a season you've passed through). What adjustments, insights, books, etc., lessened the pressure on your marriage in certain seasons?

7. If you can, share a Scripture passage that you have found especially relevant and helpful when applied to a particular season of your marriage.

8. In what ways could you prepare now for the next season of your married life?

9. The Scriptures often speak of the need to seek the counsel of others. Proverbs 15:22, for example, tells us, "without counsel plans fail, but with many advisers they succeed." How has the advice of others been beneficial?

10. As a group, what can you learn from each other about moving through different seasons of life?

homebuilders principle: Wise couples will seek the help of others who can give godly counsel about their season of life.

make a date

Set a time for you and your spouse to complete the HomeBuilders project together before the next group meeting. You will be asked at the next session to share an insight or experience from the project.

date _____ time _____

location _____

homebuilders project

On Your Own

Answer the following questions:

1. What points from the group discussion stand out in your mind as applying to your marriage?

2. In what areas do you feel you need the most help during your current marriage season?

3. What resources can you draw upon right now to help you walk through this marriage season? How can you prepare for the pressures just ahead?

4. Make a list of couples you know who have successfully completed the marital season you are now in. Consider setting a date with one of these couples to interview them on how they did it.

5. List the commitments you will have to make and the responsibilities you will have to assume to be successful in the marriage season you are now facing. Be specific.

6. Exchange study guides with your spouse. In the space provided below, compose a set of new marriage vows. Turn the commitments and responsibilities you've listed into personal promises of love and commitment to your spouse for the particular season of marriage you are facing. Be sure to include new expressions of love and appreciation!

My New Marriage Vows

With Your Spouse

1. Read your new vows to each other as an expression of fresh commitment to your marriage. Remember: every marriage season needs new vows and fresh commitments.

2. Pray together.

Remember to take your calendar to the next session for Make a Date.

5

Taking the Pressure off Sex

Understanding a spouse's needs and sacrificing to meet them are essential to a mutually rewarding sex life.

warm-up

1. How would you describe the perfect romantic evening?

2. How do you think your spouse would describe the perfect romantic evening?

3. In our research for this study, we found that many Christian men are uncomfortable talking with others about the sexual dimension of marriage. Why do you think this is more often true for men than women?

> For this session we recommend dividing into two groups— one for husbands and one for wives.

blueprints

How Pressure Affects the Sexual Relationship

Kevin and Heather struggled to keep their passion in check during their courtship and engagement. They were both Christians and were committed to purity, and they experienced the fruits of that commitment after they were married. During their first three years, they enjoyed a regular sexual relationship that was satisfying to both of them. But things began to change after they had two children within two years.

Here is a picture of home life for Kevin and Heather now, in their seventh year of marriage:

6:00–7:15 a.m.   Wake up, eat, prepare for work, feed and dress the kids.

7:15–8:00 a.m.	Kevin leaves for his thirty-minute drive to his job at a bank; Heather drops off one child at day care and another at preschool, then drives fifteen minutes to the hospital where she works as a nurse.
6:00 p.m.	Heather arrives home exhausted after picking up the kids and shopping for groceries; she starts getting dinner ready.
6:30 p.m.	Kevin arrives home with a glazed look in his eyes.
6:30–7:00 p.m.	Dinner, clean kitchen.
7:00–8:30 p.m.	Take care of the kids—games, baths, bedtime.
8:30–11:00 p.m.	Television, phone calls, catching up on unfinished work, paying bills, etc.
11:00 p.m.	Bedtime.

Kevin and Heather feel that their lifestyle is too hectic, but they don't know how to change it. It seems they rarely get a chance to spend time together the way they used to. After they finally get the kids to sleep and take care of other responsibilities, all they feel like doing is watching television or sleeping.

Both Kevin and Heather are frustrated with their sex life. He can't understand why she doesn't want to make love as much as she used to. She feels pressure to have sex more often than she wants. She resents Kevin's sex drive and wonders how he can just jump into bed and start making love when they have hardly talked to each other for days. On top of that, Heather has had trouble losing weight after bearing two children. She doesn't feel pretty, and she's hurt when he makes remarks about "losing that flab." And Kevin isn't as attracted to her anymore. Other wives lose their post-baby weight and keep their good looks, so why can't she? At the same time, Kevin isn't as trim as he used to be, either, though Heather hesitates to say anything about it.

The irony is that both are still interested in sex. But they have drifted apart; the romance is gone. It seems the only time they can get together is during the weekend, and not always then.

1. What are the main pressures and problems that Kevin and Heather are experiencing?

2. How can misunderstanding your spouse's needs create pressure in your marriage and in the sexual dimension of your relationship?

3. How has a busy schedule, with its accompanying pressure and responsibilities, affected your sexual relationship?

For Husbands

(Wives, please turn to page 58.)

Meeting Your Wife's Needs

4. Read 1 Corinthians 7:3–5, which talks about the importance of making the sexual relationship in marriage a priority. What are some practical ways you can do this?

homebuilders principle: Couples need to make their sexual relationship a high priority.

5. From your own experience, what is the most important lesson you have learned about how sex is different for a man and a woman?

6. In his book *His Needs, Her Needs,* Willard F. Harley Jr. lists
    the following needs in a marriage: admiration, affection,
    an attractive spouse, honesty and openness, family commit-
    ment, conversation, domestic support, recreational compan-
    ionship, sexual fulfillment, and financial support.

    On the chart below, rank from 1 (most important) to 5 (least
    important) how you think the men he interviewed prioritized
    these needs. Then do the same thing on the right for the
    women.

Men		Women
_____	Admiration	_____
_____	Affection	_____
_____	An attractive spouse	_____
_____	Honesty and openness	_____
_____	Family commitment	_____
_____	Conversation	_____
_____	Domestic support	_____
_____	Recreational companionship	_____
_____	Sexual fulfillment	_____
_____	Financial support	_____

Share your answers with the group, then look at the end of
this section to see how your answers match up with Harley's
findings.

7. Read 1 Peter 3:7. What are some practical ways you can show your wife honor as a woman? How can you grant her honor in this area of sex?

8. What advice would you give the man who is more interested in lovemaking than his wife is?

9. Read Philippians 2:3–4. Why is an unselfish attitude essential to a mutually fulfilling sex life? What is one thing you've done to battle selfishness in this area?

10. If appropriate, share one creative idea of how you or another person you know has added romance to the marriage relationship. (You may want to write down any good ideas that other group members contribute.)

homebuilders principle: To build true sexual intimacy, defeat selfishness by focusing on what your spouse needs.

Answer for Question 6. In Harley's book the top five needs for men were (1) sexual fulfillment; (2) recreational companionship; (3) an attractive spouse; (4) domestic support; (5) admiration. The top five for women were (1) affection; (2) conversation; (3) honesty and openness; (4) financial support; (5) family commitment.

For Wives

Meeting Your Husband's Needs

4. Read 1 Corinthians 7:3–5, which talks about the importance of making the sexual relationship in marriage a priority. What are some practical ways you can do this?

 **homebuilders principle:** Couples need to make their sexual relationship a high priority.

5. From your own experience, what is the most important lesson you have learned about how sex is different for a man and a woman?

6. In his book *His Needs, Her Needs*, Willard F. Harley Jr. lists
   the following needs in a marriage: admiration, affection,
   an attractive spouse, honesty and openness, family commitment, conversation, domestic support, recreational companionship, sexual fulfillment, and financial support.

   On the chart below, rank from 1 (most important) to 5 (least
   important) how you think the men he interviewed prioritized
   these needs. Then do the same thing on the right for the
   women.

   Men   **Women**

   _____   Admiration   _____
   _____   Affection   _____
   _____   An attractive spouse   _____
   _____   Honesty and openness   _____
   _____   Family commitment   _____
   _____   Conversation   _____
   _____   Domestic support   _____
   _____   Recreational companionship   _____
   _____   Sexual fulfillment   _____
   _____   Financial support   _____

7. Read Ephesians 5:33b. What are some practical ways you can
   show your husband respect as a man?

8. Read Philippians 2:3–4. Why is an unselfish attitude essential to a mutually fulfilling sex life? What is one thing you've done to battle selfishness in this area?

homebuilders principle: To build true sexual intimacy, defeat selfishness by focusing on what your spouse needs.

9. If appropriate, share one creative idea of how you or another person you know has added romance to the marriage relationship. (You may want to write down any good ideas that other group members contribute.)

Answer for Question 6. In Harley's book the top five needs for men were (1) sexual fulfillment; (2) recreational companionship; (3) an attractive spouse; (4) domestic support; (5) admiration. The top five for women were (1) affection; (2) conversation; (3) honesty and openness; (4) financial support; (5) family commitment.

make a date

Set a time for you and your spouse to complete the HomeBuilders project together before the next group meeting. You will be asked at the next session to share an insight or experience from the project.

date _____ time _____

location _____

homebuilders project

On Your Own

Answer the following questions:

1. Complete the following exercise to judge how you and your spouse handle the aspects of your sexual relationship. Circle the number that corresponds to your answer. Draw an X through the number you think your spouse will select.

	Low				High
The relationship we enjoy prior to lovemaking	1	2	3	4	5
Viewing sex with positive anticipation	1	2	3	4	5
The way we decide to have sex together	1	2	3	4	5
The amount of communication during lovemaking (i.e., giving feedback, expressing desires, etc.)	1	2	3	4	5
Frequency of physical intimacy	1	2	3	4	5
Gentleness and tenderness during lovemaking	1	2	3	4	5
Variety of sexual experiences together	1	2	3	4	5
Understanding of each other in this area	1	2	3	4	5

2. Read 1 Corinthians 7:3–5. Do you fully trust your spouse with your body? If not, in what aspect do you feel distrust? Why?

3. List any faulty attitudes you may have about your body or your spouse's body. Refer to Song of Solomon 5:1–16; 7:1–9.

4. Complete the following to share later with your spouse:

   • When we are sharing physical love, I like for you to . . .

   • I become discouraged when you . . .

5. What two things can you do to decrease the pressure either or both of you may feel in your sexual relationship?

6. What are the top three things you think would really please your spouse?

7. Evaluate before God whether you feel any bitterness toward your spouse regarding your sexual relationship. Read 1 John 1:9, and confess any anger or resentment that may have built up toward him or her.

With Your Spouse

1. Share your responses to the questions you answered on your own.

2. Choose three decisions you can make together that will improve your sexual relationship.

3. Schedule a whole day and night within the next month when the two of you can get away for a special time of communication and intimacy.

4. Pray together and thank God for each other as his provision for your sexual needs. Make a commitment to each other to improve your communication and intimacy.

Remember to take your calendar to the next session for Make a Date.

6

Drawing Moral
Boundaries

Defining together the living standards—on both a
biblical and a practical basis—is a key ingredient
for building a strong marriage.

warm-up

1. If a missionary couple returned to America today after
   serving in a primitive part of Africa for twenty years, what
   changes in morality would they notice in our country?

2. What changes in morality would they notice among today's
   Christians?

3. How would you explain to them the causes behind these changes?

The Slide into Moral Ambiguity

James Davison Hunter writes in his book *Evangelicalism* that words such as *worldly* and *worldliness* "have, within a generation, lost most of their traditional meanings." He asserts, "The moral boundaries separating Christian conduct from worldly conduct have been substantially undermined."

Many marriages suffer from moral ambiguity. Our world has increasingly defined right and wrong as what is right and wrong for the individual. Moral absolutes that once defined the quality and character of one's life are now being replaced with a chameleon kind of value system that has no more depth than a passing fad. A marriage built on a shifting, morally superficial foundation is clearly in trouble from the start.

1. What are some ways that you, as a Christian, feel the pressure to change your views on specific moral issues?

The good news is that a couple who takes their biblical beliefs and translates them into strong, practical statements of moral conviction will escape a host of unnecessary hurts and pressures. The result will be freedom, not confusion, and stability and unity rather than conflict and suffering.

2. Look at the concluding statement of the book of Judges (21:25). How is this statement relevant to what we are seeing in our society?

homebuilders principle: Freedom in marriage is found by embracing what is right, not in redefining what is right.

Morality and Your Marriage

3. In what specific areas do couples need to establish practical moral standards for their homes? As a group, make a collective list.

4. What can make it hard for couples to establish these standards?

5. A marriage is always in motion, either toward health or sickness, toward oneness or isolation. How can the health of a marriage be undermined by a couple's unwillingness to draw clear, practical boundaries of moral conviction?

6. What are some things you've done in your life and marriage to resist the immoral undertow of our world?

Some Considerations for Drawing Moral Boundaries

The Word of God is always the starting point in moral considerations. In some areas the Scriptures draw clear and specific moral lines. Sexual immorality, for instance, is addressed in black-and-white terms and should not be an issue in dispute. But a couple will not find so succinct a biblical statement on other issues of everyday life—issues such as the use of money, debt, work and what it takes from a marriage, the use of alcohol, the types of movies and television programs we view, time with each other and with children, etc. These, too, are moral issues with serious ramifications for any marriage.

Without sound biblical thinking and workable application in these areas and many more, the pressure of worldly conformity soon replaces "the peaceful fruit of righteousness" (Hebrews 12:11). We need to take the time and effort to think through these issues and develop our standards. Unexamined acceptance of someone else's standards sets us up for weak moral boundaries that fail under pressure.

Let's explore some biblical guidelines for drawing boundaries and convictions in these not-so-clear areas.

7. Read Titus 2:1–14. What do you think it means to "live self-controlled, upright, and godly lives in the present age"?

8. Moral conviction in a marriage will follow the pattern outlined in verse 12. Any moral boundary a couple draws for themselves should do three things:

- Make good, practical sense
- Be fair and just to all
- Meet with God's approval and harmonize with his Word

Pick one of the following situations, and determine how these guidelines help evaluate its morality:

- The husband or wife who consistently works sixty to seventy hours per week
- A spouse participating in suggestive dialogue in online chat rooms or viewing pornography on the Internet
- A couple living beyond their means and running up a huge credit card debt
- A spouse watching television shows or films that include numerous illicit sexual situations and instances of offensive language

NOTE: Some couples have had standards forced upon them by others. Then, seeking to escape this pressure, they've basically decided to avoid altogether questions about moral standards. This session is not intended to force standards upon you from the outside but to encourage you to select a definitive moral standard for yourself that harmonizes with the biblical guidelines above.

Also, one of the chief arguments against establishing clear moral standards is the cry of legalism. The goal of this session is to help you establish personal standards that you can justify and defend before the liberating Word of God. In doing so, you will find the freedom God's Word promises.

9. According to Romans 14:19, 21–22, what else needs to be considered in the moral guidelines we draw? What are some situations where you could apply this principle?

homebuilders principle: If your Christianity is not defined practically, it will be practically worthless.

10. As you look back over this entire study, what have been the highlights for you? What are the most important things you've learned?

make a date

Set a time for you and your spouse to complete the last HomeBuilders project of the study.

date _____ time _____

location _____

homebuilders project

On Your Own

Answer the following questions:

1. What pressure points do you feel in your marriage that may be the result of moral indecisiveness?

2. Consider just one area where moral boundaries are needed.

   • What practical moral lines have you drawn together about the movies you watch? The secular world has drawn its guidelines—G, PG, PG-13, R, NC-17—but how do you decide what movies you will watch? List your practical standards below. Honesty is very important here.

- What biblical guidelines did you use (if any) in establishing your standards? Do you both feel good about the standards you hold in this area?

- What pressures are associated with indecision in this area or with one person making the decisions? Who could get hurt?

- If you don't agree on these guidelines, what steps can you take to find a common moral ground you both can be accountable to uphold?

3. How do you feel about the guidelines you have drawn in the following areas? (Add to the list anything else you feel is important.) Rate your feelings using a scale of 1–5, with 1 being "uncertain, uneasy, and disturbed" and 5 being "clear, confident, and secure."

____ Care for the environment (of earth)

____ Business expense reports

____ Pornography

____ Types of entertainment

____ Use of alcohol

____ Dress

____ Paying taxes

____ Sexual freedom

____ TV/cable

____ Adultery

____ Eating

____ Gambling

____ Exaggerating

____ Abortion

____ Lying

____ Debt

____ Drugs

____ Divorce

____ My role in our marriage

____ Profanity

____ Church giving

____ Types of friends

____ Ministry involvement and our marriage

____ My spouse's role in our marriage

____ Church attendance

____ Language

____ Others:

4. In some marriages one person does not respect the other's moral boundaries and tries to nag and pressure the spouse to do things that are offensive to that person. Is this true in your marriage? If so, . . .

- is there something you can cease doing so that you would honor your spouse?

- is there something you can release your spouse to do without making him or her feel guilty?

With Your Spouse

1. Read Ephesians 4:29–32 together.

2. Go over your responses to question 2 that you answered on your own. Share your conclusions with each other. As a couple what are some standards you need to establish in this area?

3. Now look back at the list you each completed under question 3. In what areas do you need to establish guidelines as a couple? What do you think those should be?

4. At what points do you and your spouse have wide differences in opinions? Discuss those differences, seeking resolution and oneness. Remember: two must agree if they are to walk together well.

5. Share your thoughts on question 4 that you answered on your own (if applicable). Seek to resolve whatever conflicts may be there, remembering to show honor to each other (Romans 12:10).

6. How has your participation in this HomeBuilders study helped your marriage?

7. What are the most important decisions you've made?

8. Close in prayer, thanking God for the time you've spent together as a couple.

We hope that you have benefited from this study in the Home-Builders Couples Series and that your marriage will continue to grow as you both submit your lives to Jesus Christ and build according to his blueprints. We also hope that you will reach out to strengthen other marriages in your local church and community. Your influence is needed.

A favorite World War II story illustrates this point clearly.

The year was 1940. The French army had just collapsed under Hitler's onslaught. The Dutch had folded, overwhelmed by the Nazi regime. The Belgians had surrendered. And the British army was trapped on the coast of France in the channel port of Dunkirk.

Two hundred twenty thousand of Britain's finest young men seemed doomed to die, turning the English Channel red with their blood. The Fuehrer's troops, only miles away in the hills of France, didn't realize how close to victory they actually were.

Any attempt at rescue seemed futile in the time remaining. A thin British navy—the professionals—told King George VI that they could save 17,000 troops at best. The House of Commons was warned to prepare for "hard and heavy tidings."

Politicians were paralyzed. The king was powerless. And the Allies could only watch as spectators from a distance. Then as the doom of the British army seemed imminent, a strange fleet appeared on the horizon of the English Channel—the wildest assortment of boats perhaps ever assembled in history. Trawlers, tugs, scows, fishing sloops, lifeboats, pleasure craft, smacks and coasters, sailboats, even the London fire-brigade flotilla. Ships manned by civilian volunteers—English fathers joining in the rescue of Britain's exhausted, bleeding sons.

William Manchester writes in his epic novel *The Last Lion* that what happened in 1940 at Dunkirk seems like a miracle. Not only were most of the British soldiers rescued but 118,000 other Allied troops as well.

Today the Christian home is much like those troops at Dunkirk—pressured, trapped, demoralized, and in need of help. The Christian community may be much like England—waiting for professionals to step in and save the family. But the problem is much too large for them to solve alone.

We need an all-out effort by men and women "sailing" to rescue the exhausted and wounded families. We need an outreach effort by common couples with faith in an uncommon God. For too long, married couples within the church have abdicated to those in full-time vocational ministry the privilege and responsibility of influencing others.

We challenge you to invest your lives in others, to join in the rescue. You and other couples around the world can team together to build thousands of marriages and families and, in doing so, continue to strengthen your own.

Be a HomeBuilder

Here are some practical ways you can make a difference in families today:

- Gather a group of four to seven couples and lead them through this HomeBuilders study. Consider challenging others in your church or community to form additional HomeBuilders groups.
- Commit to continue building marriages by doing another small-group study in the HomeBuilders Couples Series.
- Consider using the *JESUS* film as an outreach. For more information contact FamilyLife at the number or Web site below.
- Host a dinner party. Invite families from your neighborhood to your home, and as a couple share your faith in Christ.
- If you have attended FamilyLife's Weekend to Remember marriage getaway, consider offering to assist your pastor in counseling engaged couples, using the material you received.

For more information about these ministry opportunities, contact your local church or

FamilyLife
PO Box 7111
Little Rock, AR 72223
1-800-FL-TODAY
FamilyLife.com

Every couple has to deal with problems in marriage—communication problems, money problems, difficulties with sexual intimacy, and more. Learning how to handle these issues is important to cultivating a strong and loving relationship.

The Big Problem

One basic problem is at the heart of every other problem in marriage, and it's too big for any person to deal with on his or her own. The problem is separation from God. If you want to experience life and marriage the way they were designed to be, you need a vital relationship with the God who created you.

But sin separates us from God. Some try to deal with sin by working hard to become better people. They may read books on how to control anger, or they may resolve to stop cheating on their taxes, but in their hearts they know—we all know—that the sin problem runs much deeper than bad habits and will take more than our best behavior to overcome it. In reality, we have rebelled against God. We have ignored him and have decided to run our lives in a way that makes sense to us, thinking that our ideas and plans are better than his.

> "For all have sinned and fall short of the glory of God."
> (Romans 3:23)

What does it mean to "fall short of the glory of God"? It means that none of us has trusted and treasured God the way we should. We have sought to satisfy ourselves with other things and have treated them as more valuable than God. We have gone our own way. According to the Bible, we have to pay a penalty for our sin. We cannot simply do things the way we choose and hope it will be okay with God. Following our own plans leads to our destruction.

> "There is a way that seems right to a man, but its end
> is the way to death." (Proverbs 14:12)

> "For the wages of sin is death." (Romans 6:23)

The penalty for sin is that we are separated from God's love. God is holy, and we are sinful. No matter how hard we try, we cannot come up with some plan, like living a good life or even trying to do what the Bible says, and hope that we can avoid the penalty.

God's Solution to Sin

Thankfully, God has a way to solve our dilemma. He became a man through the person of Jesus Christ. Jesus lived a holy life in perfect obedience to God's plan. He also willingly died on a cross to pay our penalty for sin. Then he proved that he is more powerful than sin or death by rising from the dead. He alone has the power to overrule the penalty for our sin.

> "Jesus said to him, 'I am the way, and the truth, and
> the life. No one comes to the Father except through
> me.'" (John 14:6)

"But God shows his love for us in that while we were still sinners, Christ died for us." (Romans 5:8)

"For the wages of sin is death, but the free gift of God is eternal life in Christ Jesus our Lord." (Romans 6:23)

The death and resurrection of Jesus have fixed our sin problem. He has bridged the gap between God and us. He is calling us to come to him and to give up our flawed plans for running our lives. He wants us to trust God and his plan.

Accepting God's Solution

If you recognize that you are separated from God, he is calling you to confess your sins. All of us have made messes of our lives because we have stubbornly preferred our ideas and plans to his. As a result, we deserve to be cut off from God's love and his care for us. But God has promised that if we will acknowledge that we have rebelled against his plan, he will forgive us and will fix our sin problem.

"But to all who did receive him, who believed in his name, he gave the right to become children of God." (John 1:12)

"For by grace you have been saved through faith. And this is not your own doing; it is the gift of God, not a result of works, so that no one may boast." (Ephesians 2:8–9)

When the Bible talks about receiving Christ, it means we acknowledge that we are sinners and that we can't fix the problem ourselves. It means we turn away from our sin. And it means we trust Christ to forgive our sins and to make us the kind of people he wants us to be. It's not enough to intellectually believe that Christ is the Son of God. We must trust in him and his plan for our lives by faith, as an act of the will.

Are things right between you and God, with him and his plan at the center of your life? Or is life spinning out of control as you seek to make your own way?

If you have been trying to make your own way, you can decide today to change. You can turn to Christ and allow him to transform your life. All you need to do is talk to him and tell him what is stirring in your mind and in your heart. If you've never done this, consider taking the steps listed here:

- Do you agree that you need God? Tell God.
- Have you made a mess of your life by following your own plan? Tell God.
- Do you want God to forgive you? Tell God.
- Do you believe that Jesus' death on the cross and his resurrection from the dead gave him the power to fix your sin problem and to grant you the free gift of eternal life? Tell God.
- Are you ready to acknowledge that God's plan for your life is better than any plan you could come up with? Tell God.
- Do you agree that God has the right to be the Lord and Master of your life? Tell God.

"Seek the LORD while he may be found; call upon him while he is near." (Isaiah 55:6)

Here is a suggested prayer:

Lord Jesus, I need you. Thank you for dying on the cross for my sins. I receive you as my Savior and Lord. Thank you for forgiving my sins and giving me eternal life. Make me the kind of person you want me to be.

The Christian Life

For the person who is a follower of Christ—a Christian—the penalty for sin is paid in full. But the effect of sin continues throughout our lives.

> "If we say we have no sin, we deceive ourselves, and the truth is not in us." (1 John 1:8)

> "For I do not do the good I want, but the evil I do not want is what I keep on doing." (Romans 7:19)

The effects of sin carry over into our marriages as well. Even Christians struggle to maintain solid, God-honoring marriages. Most couples eventually realize they can't do it on their own. But with God's help, they can succeed.

To learn more, read the extended version of this article at FamilyLife.com/HomeBuilders.

leader's notes

What is the leader's job?

Your role is more of a facilitator than a teacher. A teacher usually does most of the talking and instructing whereas a facilitator encourages people to think and to discover what Scripture says. You should help group members feel comfortable and keep things moving forward.

Is there a structure to the sessions?

Yes, each session is composed of the following categories:

Warm-Up (5–10 minutes): The purpose of Warm-Up is to help people unwind from a busy day and get to know one another better. Typically the Warm-Up starts with an exercise that is fun but also introduces the topic of the session.

Blueprints (45–50 minutes): This is the heart of the study when people answer questions related to the topic of study and look to God's Word for understanding. Some of the questions are to be discussed between spouses and others with the whole group.

HomeBuilders Project (60 minutes): This project is the unique application that couples will work on between the group meetings. Each HomeBuilders project contains two sections: (1) On your own—questions for husbands and wives to answer individually and (2) With your spouse—an opportunity for couples to share their answers with each other and to make application in their lives.

In addition to these regular features, occasional activities are labeled "Picture This." These activities provide a more active or visual way to make a particular point.

What is the best setting and time schedule for this study?

This study is designed as a small-group, home Bible study. However, it can be adapted for more structured settings like a Sunday school class. Here are some suggestions for using this study in various settings:

In a small group

To create a friendly and comfortable atmosphere, we recommend you do this study in a home setting. In many cases the couple that leads the study also serves as host, but sometimes involving another couple as host is a good idea. Choose the option you believe will work best for your group, taking into account factors such as the number of couples participating and the location.

Each session is designed as a sixty-minute study, but we recommend a ninety-minute block of time to allow for more relaxed conversation and refreshments. Be sure to keep in mind one of the cardinal rules of a small group: good groups start *and* end on time. People's time is valuable, and your group will appreciate your respecting this.

In a Sunday school class

If you want to use the study in a class setting, you need to adapt it in two important ways: (1) You should focus on the content of the Blueprints section of each session. That is the heart of the session.

(2) Many Sunday school classes use a teacher format instead of a small-group format. If this study is used in a class setting, the class should adapt to a small-group dynamic. This will involve an interactive, discussion-based format and may also require a class to break into multiple smaller groups.

What is the best size group?

We recommend from four to seven couples (including you and your spouse). If more people are interested than you can accommodate, consider asking someone to lead a second group. If you have a large group, you may find it beneficial to break into smaller subgroups on occasion. This helps you cover the material in a timely fashion and allows for optimum interaction and participation within the group.

What about refreshments?

Many groups choose to serve refreshments, which helps create an environment of fellowship. If you plan to include refreshments, here are a couple of suggestions: (1) For the first session (or two) you should provide the refreshments. Then involve the group by having people sign up to bring them on later dates. (2) Consider starting your group with a short time of informal fellowship and refreshments (15–20 minutes). Then move into the study. If couples are late, they miss only the food and don't disrupt the study. You may also want to have refreshments available again at the end of your meeting to encourage fellowship. But remember to respect the group members' time by ending the session on schedule and allowing anyone who needs to leave to do so gracefully.

What about child care?

Groups handle this differently, depending on their needs. Here are a couple of options you may want to consider:

- Have people be responsible for making their own arrangements.
- As a group, hire someone to provide child care, and have all the children watched in one location.

What about prayer?

An important part of a small group is prayer. However, as the leader, you need to be sensitive to people's comfort level with praying in front of others. Never call on people to pray aloud unless you know they are comfortable doing this. You can take creative approaches, such as modeling prayer, calling for volunteers, and letting people state their prayers in the form of finishing a sentence. A helpful tool in a group is a prayer list. You should lead the prayer time, but allow another couple to create, update, and distribute prayer lists as their ministry to the group.

Find additional help and suggestions for leading your HomeBuilders group at FamilyLife.com/HomeBuilders.

about the leader's notes

The sessions in this study can be easily led without a lot of preparation time. However, accompanying Leader's Notes have been provided to assist you when needed. The categories within the Leader's Notes are as follows:

Objectives

The Objectives focus on the issues that will be presented in each session.

Notes and Tips

This section provides general ideas, helps, and suggestions about the session. You may want to create a checklist of things to include in each session.

Blueprints Commentary

This section contains notes that relate to the Blueprints questions. Not all Blueprints questions will have accompanying commentary notes. The number of the commentary note corresponds to the number of the question it relates to. (For example, the Leader's Notes, session 1, number 5 in the Blueprints Commentary section relates back to session 1, Blueprints, question 5.)

session one

decision making and pressure

Objectives

Making wise decisions is essential in resolving the pressures that life brings.

In this session couples will

- discuss some of the typical pressures they face daily,
- understand the critical link between pressure and the decisions they make,
- learn some key principles of good decision making.

Notes and Tips

1. If you have not already done so, you will want to read the information "About Leading a HomeBuilders Group" and "About the Leader's Notes," starting on page 91.

2. As part of the first session, you may want to review with the group some ground rules (see page ix in Welcome to Home-Builders).

3. At this first meeting collect the names, phone numbers, and e-mail addresses of the group members. You may want to make a list that you can copy and distribute to the entire group.

4. Because this is the first session, make a special point to tell the group about the importance of the HomeBuilders project. Encourage each couple to make a date for a time to complete the project before the next meeting. Mention that you will ask about this during Warm-Up at the next session.

5. This session establishes a key theme in the study—that our choices can cause much of the pressure we face in life. This may be a new concept for some people who have not thought through the way they make decisions and the consequences those decisions can have. Subsequent sessions will focus on specific areas in which we need to make solid, biblical decisions. Your group members should understand that this study is not a comprehensive treatment on pressure, but it should give them a biblical framework to use as they think through pressure points in their lives.

6. You may want to offer the closing prayer yourself instead of asking others to pray aloud. Many people are uncomfortable praying in front of others, and unless you already know your group well, it may be wise to venture slowly into various methods of prayer. Regardless of how you decide to close, you should serve as a model.

7. If there is room for more people, you may want to remind the group that they can still invite another couple to join them since this study is just under way.

Blueprints Commentary

Here is some additional information about various Blueprints questions. (Note: the numbers below correspond to the Blueprints questions they relate to.) If you share any of these points, do so in a manner that does not stifle discussion by making you the authority with the real answers. Begin your comments by saying things like, "One thing I notice in this passage is . . ." or, "I think another reason for this is . . ."

3. Ryan was feeling "career pressure." He felt that he needed to be moving up the corporate ladder, that he'd be a failure if he wasn't advancing. He even thought he might be passed over in the future if he didn't take the district manager position. In addition, both Ryan and Melissa were feeling financial pressure. They had enough for their basic needs but not much more.

4. They didn't fully realize how their decision to move would change their lifestyle. They didn't have a realistic idea of what Ryan's job would involve and how it would affect them. They actually ended up with more pressure in their lives than they had before.

6. We need to seek God and his wisdom whenever we make decisions. This is the first and most important step. When facing a difficult decision, we can ask, "What would Jesus do in this situation?" The Scriptures exhort us to lead lives that are pleasing to God in all ways.

7. We are to make decisions based upon God's Word. If we obey God's Word, we will be able to withstand the inevitable pressures of life.

8. Since decisions in a marriage affect both partners, both should be involved in making the decisions. That way you get both points of view. God often puts together a man and a woman with different temperaments and decision-making approaches, and they make better decisions together than they would separately. Also, you can act as safeguards to each other to avoid bad decisions.

session two

the pressure of materialism

Objectives

Couples can reduce pressure in their marriages by taking a hard look at how they make financial decisions.

In this session couples will

- discuss the impact of materialism on financial decisions,
- take an honest look at their own materialistic attitudes,
- examine what the Bible says about materialism,
- determine some key decisions that will reduce the pressure of materialism.

Notes and Tips

1. Materialism is so pervasive in our culture that many are blind to the extent it has affected them. One of your primary tasks as leader in this session will be to gently but steadily encourage your group members to examine themselves. They may not like what they see, and they may even deny it, but the discussion should challenge them to evaluate this substantial source of pressure in their lives.

2. Some group members may be a bit defensive as they discuss materialism. For example, during the case study, which

focuses on a decision to purchase a new home, someone who has recently bought a new home may speak up and give reasons why this was a good decision. In other words, he may be justifying to the group a purchase he's recently made. If this occurs, tell the group that the main purpose of the session is to ask ourselves some difficult questions that force us to think through our values and priorities. What one couple decides is best for them may not be what another couple would decide. The key is whether a couple is submissive to God and honest with themselves about the influence of materialism in their decision.

3. Since this is the second session, your group members have probably warmed up a bit to one another but may not yet feel free to be completely open and honest about their relationships. Don't force the issue. Continue to encourage couples to attend and to complete their projects.

4. If someone in this session has joined the group for the first time, give a brief summary of the main points of session 1. Also be sure to introduce those who do not know each other. And consider giving new couples the chance to tell when and where they met.

5. If refreshments are planned for this session, make sure arrangements for them have been made.

6. If your group has decided to use a prayer list, make sure this is covered.

7. If you told the group during the first session that you'd be asking them to share something they learned from the first HomeBuilders project, be sure to ask them. This is an important way for you to establish an environment of accountability.

8. You may want to ask for a volunteer to close the session in prayer. Check ahead of time with people you think might be comfortable praying aloud.

Blueprints Commentary

1. Good clues are if the person's energies are used up in the pursuit of comfort and possessions or if the person is overly concerned with appearances and comparisons.

2. We live in a culture of consumption. We are constantly bombarded by media messages urging us to purchase things. Advertisements seduce us every day with messages designed to make us think our lives will improve if we just buy a new car, a new perfume, a new television, or even a certain brand of soft drink. It's nearly impossible to escape our culture's preoccupation with materialism.

3. Robert and Maria felt pressure from having a small house. They also felt pressure to keep up with their friends who were moving into larger homes. They were restless after being in one house for several years, and in the back of their minds was the dream home they believed would make them happy.

When they made this decision, they went from a situation where they could afford what they needed to one where they are barely keeping their heads above water. Once in the home, they felt pressure to purchase things like nicer furniture to keep up with their neighbors. And with Maria spending more time at work to help pay for the mortgage, they will feel pressure in their relationship with the children.

While some of their reasons for purchasing the new home may be good, they are too worried about how they compare with their friends. As a result, they are willing to pay a high price in terms of their family relationships and their financial security.

5. Matthew 13:18–23 says that God wants his Word to bear fruit in our lives. It's easy to allow the cares of the world and the deceitfulness of riches to choke the growth in our lives and render us fruitless.

Luke 12:15–21 tells us that life does not consist of possessions but in being rich in our faith.

First Timothy 6:6–10 is full of wisdom about finances and materialism. It tells us that we should be content with having our basic needs met. By pointing to the fact that we bring nothing into the world and will take nothing out of it, it reminds us that we should have an eternal mind-set and make pleasing God our priority. It also warns us to avoid a love for money and a desire for riches.

7. In the midst of making financial decisions, ask yourself questions like, "What would please God?" or, "Which choice would reflect a desire to seek his kingdom and his righteousness?" And be willing to act upon your convictions as you answer these questions.

Tip: If the answers from your group members are not practical enough, have them picture an actual decision they might find themselves making during the next few months (for example, purchasing clothes), and ask if they've ever considered how their decision would please God.

9. If you measure success by the quality of your relationships with God and with others, you will not be as concerned with the things you own and with the comfort of your lifestyle.

session three

the pressure of weariness

Objectives

Weariness may have less to do with the amount of work and number of activities a couple is involved with and more to do with a lack of the right kind of rest.

In this session couples will

- discuss how weariness affects marriage,
- learn how going through life without a clear sense of purpose makes one weary,
- look at whether they are using their Sundays as rest days,
- examine the burden of unconfessed sin,
- discuss what decisions they could make to release some of the activities, responsibilities, and commitments that cause weariness.

Notes and Tips

1. Congratulations. With the completion of this session, you will be halfway through this study. It's time for a checkup: How are you feeling? How is the group going? What has worked well so far? What things would you consider changing as you head into the second portion?

2. Remember the importance of starting and ending on time.

3. As an example to the group, you and your spouse should complete the HomeBuilders project for each session.

4. Greet people as they arrive. Express appreciation for their participation and support in earlier sessions.

Blueprints Commentary

5. Jesus wanted Martha to see that she was putting pressure on herself by being so busy with preparations and serving. She was driven by her self-imposed agenda, and she was missing what was most important. He helped her see that only a few things are really vital; everything else is optional.

8. David tried to conceal his sin, and his body "wasted away." He felt the heavy conviction of God on him, and this robbed him of his strength.

session four

seasonal pressures

Objectives

A wise couple will prepare for the special seasons of marriage and their unique challenges.

In this session couples will

- discuss the pressures that come with each season of marriage,
- learn about the critical need for advance preparation as each new season approaches,
- share some practical ways they learned to decrease the pressure they felt during the seasons they have already experienced.

Notes and Tips

1. Every couple is working through some stage of their married life, and nearly every couple is unprepared (at least in some ways) for what they face in that stage. It's easy to feel overwhelmed by that pressure, and it's also easy to feel isolated in each stage—as if nobody else is going through the same struggles. This session is designed for couples to encourage each other during these seasons of life. Couples will hopefully recognize that others are going through similar strug-

gles or have already experienced them and can therefore offer advice from their experience.

2. This session has a greater emphasis than others on couples sharing with other couples; you will notice less scripture and more discussion questions. Your session will succeed if you are able to create an environment where couples feel free to talk about what they are struggling with in this stage and are free to encourage others with what has helped them cope.

3. By this time group members should be getting comfortable with each other. For prayer at the end of this session, you may want to give anyone who wishes an opportunity to pray by asking the group to finish a sentence that starts something like this: *"Lord, I want to thank you for _____."* Be sensitive to those who are not comfortable doing this.

4. You may want to make some notes right after the meeting to evaluate how things went. Ask yourself questions such as, Did everyone participate? Is there anyone I should follow up with before the next session? Asking yourself questions like these will help you focus.

5. This week you and your spouse may want to write notes of thanks and encouragement to the couples in your group. Thank them for their commitment and contribution, and let them know you are praying for them. (Make a point to pray for them as you write their note.)

Blueprints Commentary

Warm-Up: Jason and Amy are facing many of the typical pressures of a couple after several years of marriage—the pressure of a growing family and the pressure of an intensive work situation. These pressures can pull a couple apart and cause isolation, or they can drive a couple to be closer—depending on how they react and adjust.

4. Proverbs 24:3–4 says we should seek God's wisdom as we build our marital "houses." And we need to be willing to follow his guidance rather than our own desires.

   Luke 14:28–30 tells us that we should plan ahead and calculate the cost as we enter new seasons of life and marriage. This means taking an honest look at the pressures and trials we're likely to face.

session five

taking the pressure off sex

Objectives

Understanding a spouse's needs and sacrificing to meet them are essential to a mutually rewarding sex life.

In this session couples will

- discuss the pressures that affect the sexual relationship,
- look at the priority of sex in marriage,
- seek to understand the differences between men and women in this area,
- discuss how they can sacrificially meet the needs of their spouse.

Notes and Tips

1. Many couples report that they feel pressure in their sexual relationship and experience intense frustration as a result. At the same time, this aspect of marriage is not always easy for people to talk about, especially men. **That's why you are splitting the husbands and wives into separate groups for this session**—to encourage more open discussion.

2. Your job as leader will be to create an environment where group members are able to loosen up a little and talk more

freely than they normally do. This doesn't mean they should share a lot of intimate details, but your willingness to talk about your marriage and the pressures you feel in the sexual relationship will be crucial in helping them relax and talk.

3. Some wives feel resentment in this area because they believe their husbands are concerned with only their own pleasure. If this attitude is expressed, especially during the discussion about meeting a spouse's needs, you might want to tell them briefly what the husbands are talking about in their discussion—the same thing!

4. Note: This session does not deal with sensitive areas such as sexual abuse, impotence, or dysfunction. However, problems such as these may surface during your discussion. Depending on the situation and how your group responds, this could offer a great opportunity for the group members to minister to each other. At the same time, watch to see whether the discussion is getting sidetracked and whether you and the group are capable of helping this person meaningfully at this time. If you sense that you need to let the session continue as originally planned, you could stop the discussion at an appropriate point and spend some time in group prayer before moving on. Then approach the person after the session and offer to meet with him or her personally—or recommend a counselor.

Blueprints Commentary

1. Kevin and Heather have an extremely busy schedule, with both partners working. When they have time to focus on

each other, they are usually exhausted and often spend that time watching television. They don't understand each other's sexual needs, and they are too concerned with outward appearance.

2. It's easy to forget that your spouse's needs are usually different from your own. It causes frustration when you expect your spouse to feel or act the same way you do. For example, a man may proceed more quickly while making love than his wife wants him to.

7. (HUSBAND) You grant your wife honor by courting her, by showing respect, by continuing to express your happiness at being her husband, by telling your children what a wonderful mother they have, by spending time with her. You can grant her honor in sex by seeking to please her.

8. (HUSBAND) First, understand the cause: a woman's feelings of insecurity or past rejection with her husband, for example, may affect her sex drive. Other inhibitors are pressure at work, fear of failure, and past sexual abuse. Second, discuss the problem as a couple, and make adjustments in your schedule. If necessary, talk to a qualified Christian counselor.

9. (HUSBAND) Wives desire pleasure in the sexual relationship just as much as husbands do. If your wife feels you are using her to gain your own gratification, she will become resentful. You should seek to please her while making love. The irony is that most men actually receive greater sexual

pleasure themselves when their wives are fully aroused, and yet they sometimes forget this and seek only to get their own pleasure out of the act.

8. (WIFE) In these verses we are commanded to consider the needs of others as more important than our own. The sexual dimension of marriage works best when both husband and wife are concerned with pleasing each other and meeting each other's needs. Note: Humility means having a proper perspective of ourselves. It doesn't mean we should deny our needs or put ourselves down. The basis of our self-worth is our identity in Christ.

session six

drawing moral boundaries

Objectives

Defining together the living standards—on both a biblical and a practical basis—is a key ingredient for building a strong marriage.

In this session couples will

- discuss how today's moral ambiguity affects them and their marriages,
- look at some scriptures that show this problem is not new,
- consider some ways to establish moral boundaries.

Notes and Tips

1. As our culture slides further and further from a biblical standard of morality, Christians are influenced by the world in ways they might not even realize. This session will help your group members confront some of these issues and will give them a framework for drawing boundaries.

2. While the Bible does not directly address some of the specific moral issues we face today—there were no movies in biblical times, for example—the Scriptures do provide guidelines we can apply to modern topics. At the same time, we need to recognize that one person's boundaries in an area (such as

movies) may differ from another's. This is not to embrace the worldly philosophy that "my morality is as good as yours." The important thing to emphasize to your group members is that they should seek to form boundaries that glorify God and harmonize with his Word.

3. People are likely to return to previous patterns of living unless they commit to a plan for continuing the progress made during this study. In this final session of the course, encourage couples to take specific steps to keep their marriages growing. For example, you may want to challenge couples to continue having a date night, as they have during this study. Also, you may want the group to consider doing another study from this series.

4. As part of this final session, you may want to devote some time to planning one more meeting—a party to celebrate the completion of this study.

5. Greet people as they arrive. You may want to comment that the time has gone quickly and that your group is already down to the last session. Begin now to plant anticipation for another study in the future.

Blueprints Commentary

Warm-Up: Someone who returns the America after twenty years would notice many changes. Among other things, he would notice that we've become a more violent and sex-saturated society. He would notice that many things that were once generally considered wrong or immoral are now accepted and even condoned. Looking closely, he would find that Christians who stand up for biblical morality are increasingly portrayed in the secular media as fanatics and bigots.

2. Everyone is doing what is right in his own eyes just as they did in this period of Israel's early history. Because people today are drifting away from God and fewer people are acknowledging his law as relevant, our culture is crumbling.

4. Many couples have not really thought through what they believe and how to apply biblical teachings to different areas of their lives. Or they may want to go on doing what they want, no matter what God's Word tells them. Or they may not be aware of how much impact a lack of definition will have on their marriage and children.

5. We are continually pressured to believe that discarding "outdated morality" will free us up to realize our true potential as human beings. In reality, the moral ambiguity of today's culture can tempt us to engage in behaviors that are destructive to ourselves and to the relations most important to us. For example, the widespread availability of pornography on the Internet can lead many men to make choices that will eventually inflict a painful or even fatal wound on their marriage relationship and on the person God has placed in their life.

9. We should consider how our actions affect other people, especially new, impressionable, or "weaker" Christians.

more tools for leaders

Looking for more ways to help people build their marriages and families?

Thank you for your efforts to help people develop their marriages and families using biblical principles. We recognize the influence that one person—or couple—can have on another, and we'd like to help you multiply your ministry.

FamilyLife is pleased to offer a wide range of resources in various formats. Visit us online at FamilyLife.com, where you will find information about our:

- getaways and events, featuring Weekend to Remember, offered in cities throughout the United States;
- multimedia resources for small groups, churches, and community networking;
- interactive products for parents, couples, small-group leaders, and one-to-one mentors; and
- assortment of blogs, forums, and other online connections.

who is familylife?

FamilyLife is a nonprofit, Christian organization focused on the mission of helping every home become a godly home. Believing that family is the foundation of society, FamilyLife works in more than a hundred countries around the world to build healthier marriages and families through marriage getaways and events, small-group curriculum, *FamilyLife Today* radio broadcasts, Hope for Orphans® orphan care ministry, the Internet, and a wide range of marriage and family resources.

Dennis and Barbara Rainey are cofounders of FamilyLife. Authors of over twenty-five books and hundreds of articles, they are also popular conference speakers and radio hosts. With six grown children and sixteen grandchildren, the Raineys love to encourage couples in building godly marriages and families.